10 spiritual lessons
you can learn from
your cat

10 spiritual lessons
you can learn from
your cat

Joanna Sandsmark

A GODSFIELD BOOK
www.godsfieldpress.com

For my mom, who is my favorite person on the planet,
Madonna Gauding, for her friendship amd support,
Brenda Rosen, for giving me a great opportunity, Nancy
Oliver and Mouse for letting me know that I don't have
the only spoiled cat in the world, and Trace and Ilsa for
being some of the best friends and teachers I ever had.

First published in Great Britain in 2004
by Godsfield Press,
a division of Octopus Publishing Group Ltd
2–4 Heron Quays
Docklands
London E14 4JP

2 4 6 8 10 9 7 5 3

Printed and bound in China

ISBN 1 84181 240 4
EAN 9781841812403

Contents

Introduction

Several years ago, I decided to get a kitten. A local pet adoption service was holding an adoption day at a local pet shop. As each new batch of kittens came in, I looked them over eagerly. I talked to them, held them, cuddled and waited for a sign. Nothing. Where was my cat?

After hours of looking, I sat down on some sacks of food, despondent. I could have sworn my cat was supposed to be there. As I debated going home, I looked up. Clinging to the wire of her cage was a tiny black kitten with a white stomach, four white paws and a paintbrush tail. I had never seen a tail like it. This black tail had a bright white tip, and inside the tip was a coal black centre. I watched as this tiny acrobat climbed the walls of her cage, reaching for the wire ceiling. The rest of her litter mates were fast asleep, but this little one would have none of that.

I asked to hold her. The instant she touched my hands, I knew she was mine and I was hers. Where other kittens had squirmed, this one snuggled and purred. Where others looked at me like a stranger, she looked at me as an old friend. Time to go.

But something held me there: the most adorable face I'd ever seen in my life. A little greyish puffball with black-and-white striping, she resembled her sister in many ways. She had four white paws and a puff of white (without the drama) on the end of her tail. Her eyes were huge and they stared at me, watching my every move.

I asked to hold her. What was I thinking? I had come for *one* cat. And now I had two, and I didn't know which was my kitten because they both claimed me, they both purred and cuddled, they both looked at me with unconditional love.

'Take them both,' said a female voice.

I looked up to see the woman from the adoption service.

'Oh, no. I just want one,' I said quite firmly.

'Yes, but we need people to give foster homes to the kittens in between adoption days. If you keep the extra until next weekend, you'd be doing us a big favour.'

You're laughing at me. But I was so blindly in love that I was willing to believe anything, as long as I could take them both. So I agreed. *Just* a week. I signed the papers for both. Paid for both (donation, refundable next weekend). Got supplies for both. But I was only going to keep one. Yup.

I called a friend, told him what I had done, and he said, 'I can't believe you got *two* cats!'

'I have one, the other is a foster cat.'

He just laughed.

Later that night he called, asking me how many kittens I had. 'Just one, but I can't figure out which one. The lady said taking both would help me decide, but it's really tough.'

The next morning he called again, asking me how many kittens I had. 'Two. I was a fool. Leave me alone.'

It was probably the least foolish thing I've ever done. Trace (the black cat with the dramatic tail) and Ilsa (the world's sweetest face) and I (the human) spent years of bliss together. Sadly, Ilsa passed away in December of 2000. But Trace and I are still together.

I realized early on that the cats were not pets; they were teachers. We were put together to learn from each other, and to add generous doses of love to each and every day of our lives. This book is my way of passing on those lessons, on the off chance that other cats aren't as talkative.

Trace and Ilsa showed me how to stick to a hunt and capture the prize, whether it was a much-desired project, a good job or wonderful new friends. Like all cats, they had remarkable powers of healing, and I learned about courage in the face of adversity by watching Ilsa fight two power-ful, fatal diseases at once, without ever giving up her gentle, loving nature.

They taught me how to make a leap without falling, how to purr when I was happy, and how to shed those things that are no longer serving me. In short, Trace and Ilsa made me a better person. I hope their lessons will help you in your spiritual journey, as they did me. And if you have any questions on the material, just ask your cat.

We are continually faced by great opportunities brilliantly disguised as [seemingly] unsolvable problems.
LEE IACOCCA, AMERICAN INDUSTRIALIST (B. 1924)

The cat's eye

The cat is sound asleep, seemingly oblivious to the world around her. Suddenly she wakes, alert, her senses keen. She stares at a fixed point on the wall – but nothing is there! Maybe to my eyes there is nothing, but she is focused and stealthy as she approaches. Like a lion tracking a zebra, she cautiously places one paw in front of the other, stalking the wall. After staring at it, sniffing, cocking her ears forward, she slowly, tentatively, reaches out one paw and touches the air, as if assuring herself the invisible object is real.

What does she see that I can't? Is it ancient Egypt's cat-god, Bast? Is it a ghost, or a phantom? Is it an insect so tiny I can't find it? Is the corner of my room a portal to another dimension and she is bravely keeping the interlopers out of our world?

I wish I could ask her. But that would probably prompt her to ask me why I stare at white pages of wonderfully chewable paper (paper being one of the four basic food groups for many cats) with all the black squiggles on it. I think it's best that instead of questioning or doubting our cats, we learn from them. They have so much to teach us.

Sharpening your senses

It's easy to get complacent when using our senses. We learn to be selectively sighted. For example, when you open your wardrobe, do you really see each article of clothing? Or do you see the things you wear most often, blind to the off-sized or unstylish choices of yesteryear? 'I don't have anything to wear!' you might say to a closet full of clothes.

Do you hear every sound? We deafen our senses to the background noises of familiar places. The hum of the refrigerator or the ticking of the clock – we don't hear them unless we consciously think to do so.

Like us, cats memorize their environment. It's their territory, and they must know it intimately in order to protect it. If anything new enters their world, they explore it with all of their senses. My cat is particularly fond of exploring the handbags of female guests. Smart enough to know that the bag itself is not the only new thing in her world, she must also inspect the contents. I do a lot of apologizing to guests.

Both cats and humans tend to know what is in their territory. But unlike humans, cats will make frequent trips to check on everything. You know what's in the linen closet and don't need to open the door every few days to check. But your cat has to make sure that everything is the same in there as it was before. He probably asks you to open the door (or does it himself), and will most likely just take a quick look and sniff, then walk away. This is behaviour we can learn from.

Looking into your mental linen closet

To check your inner spaces, you may not have to change your physical world (unlike me, who really needs to do a good cleaning). But when is the last time you paid close attention to your spiritual world? I'm not talking about religion, though it can certainly include that, but rather your own sense of right and wrong, your morals, your opinions, your connection to your higher self and the universe around you.

I love my cats because I love my home,
and little by little they become its visible soul.

JEAN COCTEAU, POET, WRITER, ARTIST AND FILM-MAKER (1889–1963)

It's easy to carry in your mind mental linen closets that are filled with familiar thoughts and ideas, and yet never look at them with new eyes. You might not check them regularly to see if they are serving you, or inspect them for subtle changes. How often do you see the invisible things in the corner? Things like latent prejudices, outdated attitudes or child-hood teachings that don't fit your life. Yet these things can stay with you forever, unless you really *see* them for what they are.

Your mind and your spirituality are your most basic – and most important – territory. They deserve the kind of attention that your cat gives to hers. Make a mental map of your attitudes, and see if any of them present a danger. Inspect your fears, and perhaps you'll discover that they have been holding you back from the things you most desire. Search for shame, doubt and uncertainty, as they can undermine any progress you make.

Don't be afraid to stare at your inner life with a cat's eyes, and if you find things that threaten your health, happiness and success – fight them with everything you have. Your cat will do his level best to protect you from those inter-dimensional invaders in the corner. It's up to you to protect yourself from the fears, shames and doubts that can keep you from living the life you want.

Watch a cat when it enters a room for the first time. It searches and smells about, it is not quiet for a moment, it trusts nothing until it has examined and made acquaintance with everything.

JEAN JACQUES ROUSSEAU, POLITICAL PHILOSOPHER, EDUCATIONIST AND ESSAYIST

(1712–1778)

Exercise: **Exploring your territory**

Discover what's there, in your inner life. Close your eyes and pick out every sound you can hear. Try to hear what you've never noticed before. Open your eyes and look at your familiar environment as if you've never seen it before. Look for shapes or motion or anything you can imagine (like shadows in the dark when you were a kid).

Now travel inward and look in the less-travelled places in your mind. Think about the things that keep you from achieving what you want in life. Is it fear? Shame? Doubt? Are there old ideas that no longer fit, like that outdated shirt that's too small for you, still hanging in your closet? Are you carrying a childhood trauma, or words shouted in anger, or the goals of your parents instead of yourself?

Try to see these obstacles. You don't have to do any more right now. Just shine a light on them. You can't excise demons if you don't know they're there. If you find things, write them down. We'll talk about conquering them later.

Lesson 2

Dogs have masters; cats have partners

Some of your cat's behaviour might seem strange. Why does she like high places? Why does she want doors opened, when she has no interest in going through them? Why does she get upset if another cat even comes near the house?

The answers are usually found in the natural instincts a cat uses to survive in the wild. Unlike dogs, which live in packs, non-domesticated cats are solitary creatures that hunt alone in a large, single cat territory.

They like high places because they are good vantage points from which to survey their domain. This holds true in the wild or in your living room. Cats keep a mental map of their territory and must check it constantly to make sure it hasn't changed. The presence of another cat skirting the edges of what a cat considers his territory is a threat. He will instantly hiss and puff up his fur to say, 'I'm big; I'm mean; you do *not* want to cross me!'

Yet even these isolationists aren't truly without the support of their community. When a female cat has a litter, other females will often act as midwives and babysitters for her kittens. Males will keep predators and other males away from the babies. No cat is truly an island.

Being a social animal

People are social animals, yet it can be easy to isolate yourself. Whether you are alone in a crowd, living in a large city without knowing the people on the other side of your walls, or alone in the country, miles from the nearest neighbour, modern life can impose a solitary existence.

Or maybe you're in the opposite situation. Perhaps you are so enmeshed in your social groups or family that you never have a moment to yourself. The cacophony of constant voices deafens your thoughts, and needy eyes watch your every move until you just want to run away.

Both situations are challenging. It's uncomfortable to be so isolated that you never see or speak to anyone for long stretches of time. Under those conditions, it's easy to feel so independent and self-reliant that you are unprepared when something goes wrong. You have no support system in place. There's no one to turn to. And that can mean genuine danger.

Cats prefer to be at great heights so they can look down
at dogs, humans and other lower life forms.

ANONYMOUS

You can make more friends in two months by becoming interested in other people than you can in two years by trying to get other people interested in you.

DALE CARNEGIE, INDUSTRIALIST (1888–1955)

24

But it can be just as dangerous to rely too heavily on your family and friends. Eventually, it becomes difficult to do anything on your own. And you find yourself so dependent on others that you lose the self-esteem that comes from self-reliance.

Finding the balance

Your feline friend knows that a good amount of independence is the cat's meow. But she also knows when to ask for things, such as food, water, brushing or play. The important thing is the balance. You need to have both self-reliance and a social support system in your life.

How do you find that balance? Start small, but work steadily towards the goal. If you've found yourself to be alone too much, you need to consciously make choices that will put you in places where others are, and where friendships can grow. For example, taking an adult education class is an excellent way to get out of the house, improve your mind or skills and meet new people.

Voluntary work is a way to meet people and help your community. Get involved with a political campaign. It's a great way to find people who share your views of the world. Your religion is a wonderful place to make friends. Join a committee, and attend services regularly. Perhaps you have a hobby. That's a perfect chance to meet people who share your interests.

There are many resources for finding people, including libraries, online communities and community centres – the list is nearly endless. The important thing is not to starve your spirit by always being alone and isolated.

The opposite situation, an overcrowded life, is a little more difficult to solve. When you get used to relying on others, or find you have no time for yourself, it's difficult to carve out the space you need to rediscover your own thoughts. Difficult, but very necessary!

If you're a stay-at-home mother whose life is filled with demands from your children and spouse, it's imperative to capture some time that belongs only to you. You'll need help – from your spouse, your family, your community or maybe just a babysitter – but it's essential for you to spend some time thinking of yourself first.

The important thing, whether you're alone or in a crowd, is to find a healthy balance. You need moments when you're laughing and talking and sharing with others. You also need moments when you can think quietly, read a book, watch some television, take a walk or be pampered at a spa. A healthy spirit is one that is fed from within and without.

Exercise: **Taking the first steps**

Think about the balance between self-reliance and dependency. Work out where you fall on the continuum. Write a list of six things you can do to find a better balance. If you feel isolated, they might be things like 'go to a class', 'host a party' or 'make plans with friends'. Concentrate on things that will lead to social interaction. If you rely too heavily on others, they might be things like 'balance my own chequebook, 'take a day trip alone' or 'see a movie by myself'. Think of things that will foster a more independent spirit.

Pick one of the things on the list and make it happen. How did it feel? Did you have fun? Was it difficult? Write about your experience, focusing on any benefits you derived from the activity. If you feel you broke through a mental barrier with the first item, move on to the next. If you don't feel you made any progress, look for an item on your list that appears challenging. Do that one next. Remember, if you do the most difficult ones first, the rest should be easy!

Lesson 3
Play with your toys

My cats, Trace and Ilsa, had very individual tastes in toys. As a kitten, Trace liked chasing and fetching little plastic rings, often found on bottles of milk. Ilsa liked stringy objects such as ribbons, ropes, elastic – basically anything she could catch, hold and chew on. When I would buy a new toy, one or the other would claim it (apparently without jealousy, one of the things that separates the animal kingdom from most human siblings) and the other would leave it alone.

One of Trace's favourite toys was imbued with magic. It was an old, worn-out canvas catnip sack (that had long ago lost its catnip) with a fuzzy fake mouse coming out of the top. She would carry it around and cry whenever I wasn't there. When I came home, I would find it on one of my favourite places to sit, like the couch or the computer chair. I am convinced that the toy was placed there to make me magically appear. Eventually, I always did, so I guess it worked. Never discount cat magic.

Their favourite toys had great value to both of them. They understood the need to play, and the closeness it can bring between cat and human. Just be sure you don't miss the message your cat is sending – humans, like cats, need to play.

Sports

In this frantic, bustling world, it's easy to lose sight of the fact that play is necessary for your health. Cats use play to hone their hunting skills. You can use play to help shape many aspects of your equivalent 'hunting skills' – your body, mind and spirit.

Team sports, for example, are an excellent way to keep in shape and have social interaction. You can bond with team-mates, make new friends, get physically fit, let out aggression in a safe environment, and have an excuse to eat pizza afterwards.

Individual sports also have many advantages. Whether it's golf, tennis or bowling, it usually involves some physical exertion, a friend or two, and a great time. Add bonus points if you get some fresh air and break into a sweat. Whatever sport you choose, team or individual, put your focus on having fun.

Games

But sports aren't the only way to have a good work-out. It's just as important to test your mind. Personally, I am always joyful when I'm with a group of friends playing a party game. Win or lose (and I'll admit I always play to win), the laughter, the camaraderie, the testing of one's knowledge, skills and luck, is impossible to resist.

Some people cheat themselves out of these experiences because they're 'no good at it' or 'never win'. With all the positive benefits of sports and games, it is impossible not to be a winner on some level, so don't allow that defeatist mind-set to deter you. Declare yourself a winner if you laugh, feel your heart pumping or even just participate.

Relaxation

Another use for games and toys is relaxation. After working a full day, it's important to have something that will allow you to let the stresses of the day seep out. It might be playing with your kids, watching TV, reading a book or tinkering with a hobby – all are excellent sources of stress relief.

Cats who don't get enough play often become bored and lethargic. As their owner, playing with your pet is as much of a responsibility as feeding

No matter how much pressure you feel at work, if you could find ways to relax for at least five minutes every hour, you'd be more productive.

DR JOYCE BROTHERS, PSYCHOLOGIST AND AUTHOR (B. 1949)

her or changing her litter. Be just as responsible with yourself. Don't allow yourself to become so bogged down with worry, fear, tension and stress that you lose all the joy in your life.

It is essential that you laugh and smile every day. It is good for your heart to relax and have fun. It is, in fact, a health issue in every way. You'll live longer, will have much better health, and will be a better companion to your loved ones. In short, you now have the perfect excuse to be silly!

Sports and games also enrich you spiritually. Self-knowledge is a primary key to spiritual growth. From games, you can learn things about yourself, such as how you think and react. You can even find hidden or arcane knowledge that you didn't know you had. In many ways, a game is like a tiny metaphor for how you tackle the challenges in your life. That's valuable information, and can lead to spiritual discoveries of profound depth.

No one is advocating that you put aside your responsibilities so that you can spend your life playing. But without the occasional playful escape, you might find yourself unable to cope with the stresses of your daily life. Steal a couple of hours and sweat a little, laugh a little, think a little, play a little — and you'll find yourself better equipped to handle the serious issues that might arise.

Exercise: **Time to play!**

It's playtime; have fun. There are a number of wonderful party games on the market, or in that cupboard you rarely visit. Plan a games night with friends or family, and leave both your inhibitions and your daily worries at the door. Find a game with rules that are easy to understand, and where all the players have an equal chance of winning. Team games are especially fun, such as Pictionary. Make sure you have the right number of players for the game, as well. And finally, be prepared to do a lot of laughing.

Next, plan a day of sports, say a tennis round robin, or a day of swimming at the beach or the pool. If you can manage it, getting a big group of friends together for a picnic and a team sport is a fantastic way to spend a Saturday. It's like having a mini-holiday without ever leaving home.

Be sure to arrange the next day of gaming or sports before you say your goodbyes.

When I play with my cat, who knows if I am not a pastime for her

more than she is to me?

MICHEL DE MONTAIGNE, ESSAYIST (1533–1592)

35

Lesson 4

Cat got your tongue?

Scientists say that animals might have a clear ability to communicate. Pet owners have known that for centuries! Trace doesn't just tell me when she wants something, she clearly tells me exactly what it is that she wants.

'I want to be brushed' is completely different from 'I need food', as is 'Play with me' different from 'Give me some cuddling'. Unlike most humans, she's never shy about asking for what she wants. She can, in fact, be quite relentless in her search for satisfaction.

Clear communication

Are you as clear in your communication when you have something to say? Most likely you take the human route, hiding some of your needs in mazes of language that diffuse the intent. I understand – it's tough to take the risks that can sometimes accompany frankness.

The problem arises when it is something important to you. That's when you can't take the chance that your voice won't be heard. It is imperative that you speak with both clarity and strength. You've probably heard the phrase 'choose your battles'. If it is indeed a battle worth fighting, you need to be armed and dangerous. Not with pointy things (we'll have no bloodshed here), but with words.

Words are powerful tools, and there are certain things you can do to improve your chances – even if you have the habit of freezing up, or never feel you can express yourself clearly. Here are just a few suggestions.

Avoid speaking from anger

Anger is probably the biggest destroyer of clear communication. It makes you say things you'll regret – things you may not even mean. It's just that you're so… so… *angry*! Sometimes it can't be avoided, but on those occasions when you have a choice, take time to cool down before you respond to, or confront, the person who angered you. One trick is to write down what you want to say, but don't let anyone see it. Just let some of the steam out. A calm, reasoned response to a situation has a better chance of communicating than statements filled with vitriol.

*To effectively communicate, we must realize that we are all different
in the way we perceive the world and use this understanding as a guide
to our communication with others.*

ANTHONY ROBBINS, AUTHOR AND SPEAKER (B. 1960)

Remember, your goal shouldn't be to hurt someone. There are few things more damaging to your spirit than deliberately harming another soul. Instead, make your goal the clear communication of your own feelings and views. By taking anger out of the equation, you'll find a marked improvement in your communication.

Think things through before you speak

Let's say you want to ask your boss for more money. Don't just run into his office and blurt it out. You'll be unprepared for any questions he might ask, or problems he might cite. It's always better to think things through first, and to anticipate what the other person might say. Then you won't have to rely on quick thinking from a possibly frozen brain.

Find the focus

When someone hurts you, do you tend to focus on blaming that person, rather than speaking from your own hurt? If so, this could be a reason why confrontations don't always go your way, despite your being in the right.

I once had a friend who was manipulating me into doing her favours. I sat her down, and spoke about how I felt when she said certain things. I never used the word 'manipulate' (it's a loaded word, full of accusation and, therefore, something to be avoided). I focused only on my feelings. When I finished, she said, 'Oh no, I've been manipulating you! That's terrible!'

She hadn't realized what she had been doing, yet she was able to recognize it when I told her how I felt. Instead of becoming an argument and the end of a friendship, that conversation brought us closer together. Even if you fear confrontation, if you use this method, it avoids many of the unpleasant outcomes.

Pick your battles

I know I mentioned this before, but it bears repeating. Don't fight everything. If you are constantly battling about the small things, you risk being ignored when something important happens.

Sometimes, you are aware of injustices. It might be towards you, or it might be towards someone else. Don't let fear stand in the way of speaking up. Be as bold as your cat when she wants to be fed. Be clear, concise and true to your cause.

A healthy spirit is an expressive one. You've probably felt that wonderful sensation of a weight lifting off of your shoulders when you finally say what you had been keeping inside. Feed that healthy spirit within you with clear communication that is never meant to hurt, but instead, serves your best interests.

Exercise: **Civil communication**

Look at how you communicate, or don't, with others. Think of the last time you kept your opinions silent, yet wanted to speak. Write down what you wish you'd said. Now rewrite it in a way that removes any anger or bitterness, clearly states the problem and presents a solution.

Now think of a time when you spoke in anger, possibly hurting someone with sharp, bitter words. What could you have said in that situation that would have communicated your feelings without hurting the other person?

Over the next two weeks, try to recognize all the times when clear communication is called for. Do your best to implement the lessons you've just read. Thank your cat the next time he meows at you.

Lesson 5

Take a catnap

The sight of a languid cat in a sunny window is enough to bring envy to the heart of any human who can't find five minutes to let go of the day's worries. Cats are masters of the art of napping, and they sleep 16–18 hours per day. Being carnivores, they have the luxury of being able to rest for long periods because they don't require a constant food source as herbivores do. It's good to be king of the jungle (or queen of the windowsill).

Most likely, you don't spend your day grazing on low-yield grasses and shoots, so you, too, are built for solid sleeping. But on the modern roller coaster, it isn't always easy to get in your eight hours, let alone do quality napping or relaxation. Yet doctors are forever telling us about the importance of sleep – and for good reason. Sleep is when you recharge your batteries, mentally review your day through dreams, and rest your physical body, including your heart and lungs.

Delta sleep

There are several stages of sleep. You've probably heard of REM (rapid eye movement) sleep. That's the dreaming stage and much has been written about it. But the sleep stage where you get the most rest is the Delta phase. That's when your heart and breathing slow down, and your brainwave patterns change dramatically. Instead of the frantic dreaming of REM, your brain slows to a crawl in Delta. This is what your body is craving when you're sleep-deprived or over-tired. Everything just wants to shut down for a while so that it can stop working so hard.

If you are sleep-deprived, you lose function in body, mind and soul. Your spirit is like a TV antenna that isn't pointed towards a signal — full of static with only random flashes of sound and picture. And because you can't hook your spirit up to a cable or a dish, you need to do the fine-tuning yourself.

REM sleep

As much as your body and mind need the Delta sleep, that's also how much your spirit needs the REM sleep. There are many books and complex theories written on the meaning of dreams. To discuss them all would be impossible, so let's look at the basics.

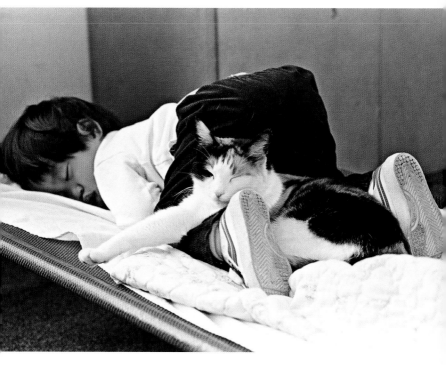

In my experience, cats and beds seem to be a natural combination.

LOUIS J. CAMUTI, DOCTOR OF VETERINARY MEDICINE (1893–1981)

Dreaming permits each and every one of us to be quietly and safely insane every night of our lives.

WILLIAM DEMENT, SLEEP SPECIALIST, PROFESSOR AT STANFORD UNIVERSIY (B. 1929)

Does your cat dream? Your cat has the same stages of sleep that you do, including REM. When she is in that stage, you'll often see her feet twitching, and you might hear some meows or grunts. You can see that she is dreaming.

Dreaming

Everyone dreams, but not everyone remembers their dreams. You have the greatest chance of remembering them if you are awakened during REM. Once you slip back into one of the other stages of sleep, most of your dreams will fade from your memory. There are exceptions, of course, but this works as a general rule.

Are dreams the voice of your spirit? Now we're getting into the tricky stuff. Scientists who study the mind say that dreams are a rehashing of your day. They'll pick up different elements of the things you dealt with and review them. Sounds very practical, doesn't it?

There is another school of thought that points to a complex pattern of symbols, colours, numbers, images, locations and characters that show deeper meanings than mere summaries of the day. These dream interpretations include a very spiritual aspect.

If the latter theories are true, and your dreams are there to help guide you through life, then the importance of sleep is about far more than rest for your mind and body. Dream interpreters postulate that dreams can teach you about your health, your state of mind, your spirit – in short, they can help to guide you towards good decisions.

Perhaps this is why cats seem so balanced and independent. They may already know about the importance of dreams. Their constant napping may be a cleansing ritual as necessary as their grooming.

Relaxation

As important as sleep is, you need more than that. You also need to find time each day to relax – conscious, but tranquil. From the high-powered business executive to the stay-at-home mother, everyone needs to step away from pressure and responsibility. Most likely, you'll want something *different* from what you've been doing all day.

There are a lot of ways to relax. We talked about sports and games in Lesson 3; both are excellent forms of relaxation through stimulation. Relaxing doesn't just mean sitting in a chair not doing anything. Relaxing is whatever you respond to as a release from your day.

A cat sleeps fat, yet walks thin.

FRED SCHWAB, *THE LAST DAMN CAT BOOK*

You can watch television, climb a mountain, play on the computer, bake a cake, go out to dinner, listen to music, paint a picture, play football, read a book – it's your choice. Only you know what activities, or non-activities, you find relaxing. Just make sure that you build in time each day to participate in something you find enjoyable and stress-free.

Exercise: **Some time for yourself**

Allow yourself to relax. Tell anyone who might interrupt you that you need 20 minutes to yourself. If the weather is warm, go outdoors. Feel the warmth of the sun, and the texture of the grass. Listen to the buzzing of insects, and the ambient sounds. Smell the loamy scent of earth and flora. Now let your muscles relax and your mind drift. If the weather doesn't allow this, go to a room where you can be undisturbed; find a comfortable chair or sink into a hot bath; let your muscles relax and your mind drift. Make sure your worries stay on the other side of the door.

If you prefer stimulation when you relax, target your time towards a favourite activity. Work out at the gym, play a sport or go for a long walk. If you prefer a mental workout, do a crossword puzzle, read a good book or play a computer game.

Lesson 6
Keep one eye open

Sometimes, cats sleep with one eye open. This allows them to react quickly to danger or opportunity. You can achieve great things if you, too, adopt this one-eyed mindfulness.

It's easy to drift through life, drowsily going about routines. It's familiar. You're used to the way your typical day works out. You probably have certain expectations and habits that are so comfortable, change would be upsetting. It's easier to ignore, fear or shun new things.

Instead of walking through life with both eyes closed, be more like your cat. Keep one eye open. Be mindful of the world around and within you. With awareness comes opportunity.

Opportunities, large and small

When you hear the word 'opportunity' you might think about a promotion or a new job. Widen your thoughts. Think instead of all opportunities.

Be aware that there could be chances to improve every aspect of your life. Whether it's work and relationships, or your own body, mind, heart and soul, the seeds are riding the wind currents. It's up to you to notice their flight.

One of the wonderful things about your spiritual life is that it can be enriched through many means, not just through direct thought or action. Eating more healthily improves the body, but it's just as good for your spirit. Helping those in need strengthens the heart and mind, but it's especially fruitful for your higher self. Getting a promotion may ease financial burdens, but it also enriches your spirit.

All of these, and more, happen if you are open to new possibilities and take advantage of opportunities that present themselves. Watch your cat when he stalks a bird or chases an insect. He doesn't wait for them to come to him, he pursues them with stealth and purpose. His movements are deliberate, practical and dangerously beautiful. His eyes are clear, watching every move his prey makes. He pounces with energy and grace, and if he misses, he continues the chase. What a perfect way to approach a sudden opportunity!

Be as aggressive as he is. Don't just watch the opportunity, wishing it would hop to within arm's reach. Give it your focus and your energy. The

Any cat who misses a mouse pretends it was aiming for the dead leaf.

CHARLOTTE GRAY, AUTHOR

more important it is to you, the more you need to invest in making sure your hunt is successful. If it is truly what is best for you, it will happen.

But what if you are frustrated, thinking, 'I don't see any opportunities now'. There's no need to lie dormant in a 'waiting place' – hoping something happens to walk within your focus. Some of the best opportunities are the ones that you create yourself.

Creating opportunities

Let's say you love drawing, and want to become a professional artist. Doodling at your desk probably won't get you discovered. To be an artist, you would have to put yourself and your work into the places where opportunities can arise.

You'd need to have more than just talent; you'd also need skills. So you go to some classes, meet other artists, are taught by a teacher who knows something about the art world, and you learn. You work hard, building a good portfolio. You learn who's who in your area, or move to a place with a large art community. You attend the functions where these people are, you make phone calls, you send your résumé and samples to businesses, and you contact galleries.

During this process you'll learn about the art world, your craft and the business of art. But you'll also learn perseverance, and improve your social skills and confidence. You'll imbue your work with the messages of your soul, and enrich it through your talent. You'll learn to part with the 'best piece I've ever done' realizing that your true best is yet to come.

Then one day, when you aren't expecting it, an opportunity will fall in your lap. Or it might seem that way until you realize how many things you did, how many lessons you learned, how much energy you used, to get your lap to the very place where an opportunity 'happened' to be.

That's the reality of most opportunities – and isn't it wonderful? They're usually not 'out of the blue'; things that are just handed to you so that you'll never learn, grow or appreciate them. And the more opportunities you create, the more you'll realize how abundant they are. Even the obstacles in your path can become the best things that ever happened to you, if you face them with spiritual growth in mind.

In the end, the measure of your life will be based on what you've done, whom you loved, who loved you, and whether your contribution to the world was positive or negative. But the measure of your soul will be the lessons you learned, and the spiritual opportunities you refused to waste.

Exercise: **Be on the lookout**

Throughout the following week, pay attention to all opportunities that present themselves. It can be large or small, like a chance to better yourself in your line of work, an opportunity to open a door for someone struggling with parcels, or a moment to have a deeper than usual discussion with a loved one. Try to pay special attention to things that you might ordinarily have avoided. How many new opportunities did you see? How many were you able to take advantage of? How did this new mindfulness of the world around you feel?

With these questions in mind, spend the next week creating a new opportunity. Ideas or inspiration can come from anywhere. For example, you might read a newspaper story about loneliness at a retirement home, and decide to spend a day visiting the elderly residents. You might learn some extraordinary things about history, events and interesting people. Whatever you do, make it something that you personally want in your life. It's your opportunity, so have a great time creating it!

Lesson 7

Make the leap

love to watch Trace when she's about to make a perilous jump. She gets a look of supreme concentration in her eyes, focusing on her target with grim intensity. Her back end wiggles as she settles her muscles, building up the spring-loaded force necessary for her jump to have the distance she needs. Then, in an explosion of muscle, she stretches her body into the air, front paws seeking safety. Her landing is usually surprisingly soft and delicate. It's just a whisper of paws and a nonchalant stroll across the new surface.

I remember watching this one day when I was feeling a bit down, and I wished I had her confidence and grace. I wondered what had been important enough to have risked that dangerous jump. Then with a nuzzle on my hand, I realized I was her target. She had made her perilous leap to be closer to me. It seemed she had far more courage than her owner. What exactly was keeping me from making my own leaps?

Think before you leap

One reason cats jump the way they do is because they know the odds are high that if they miss, they will land on their feet. It's not a bad way to think about your own leaps, is it? Some time should be spent thinking about landing — both on top if you succeed, and on the ground if you should fail.

An excellent method to use to do this is visualization. See yourself in your mind's eye making the successful leap. Anticipate the actions you'll take to keep your aim true, and then consider what steps should be made if you succeed. Will you land softly and continue your life's journey? Will you find yourself hanging on to a precipice, trying to pull yourself up that last short distance? Or will you miss the target entirely and have to start from scratch?

Make some contingency plans. Try to anticipate problems, and their possible solutions, so that if surprised, you can deal with them. When you've visualized many possibilities, you'll have the tools to do so.

And if you fall? Don't just visualize what you'll need to do to land on your feet, try to see how you can leap again. Maybe you needed a better angle, or a higher position or a more solid platform from which to jump.

In other words, don't be unrealistic; be ready to do the work. Your cat may be capable of jumping from the floor to the top of the bookshelf. But if there is a handy chair that cuts the distance in half, she'll happily use that as her launch pad.

Say goodbye to doubt

How do you get rid of all the negative baggage you've accumulated in your life? One method is to visualize those thoughts and issues as beasts or monsters. For example, Doubt might be a large, hairy creature with smothering arms and empty eyes. It's very difficult to jump at opportunities with this massive brute clinging to your body, pulling you down and holding you back. Doubt simply has to go. How do you do that?

First, you thank him. After all, he wouldn't exist if you had never asked him to. He's your creation. He is there because you needed him at one time in your life, and he has served you faithfully since his inception.

'Thank you, Doubt, you've done a great job. You protected me from making some stupid decisions. You kept me safe when I might have done something too risky. You held on tight when I might have become cocky. I appreciate all that you've done for me, Doubt.'

Prepare to feel a bit idiotic when you do this. After all, you're talking to 'Doubt' here, and he'll do his best to make you doubt your own sanity for talking to an imaginary monster. Do it anyway. Kids talk to imaginary things all the time, why shouldn't you?

Okay, you've had your little chat with Doubt. Now it's time to send him on his way, because he is no longer serving you.

'Goodbye, Doubt. You need to go. There are risks I must take. I need to feel good about myself. I need to reinvest the power I've given you to my new friend, Belief.'

Visualize Doubt walking out of the door, and out of your life. Put him in a cab, on a horse, on a rickshaw – anything you want – and watch until he disappears. Then welcome your new friend, Belief. Perhaps Belief is a knight in shining armour, or a pair of glistening wings on your back or an ornate, golden mirror. It's your friend; you create it. And as long as Belief is with you, you are safe from Doubt.

It will be an ongoing thing. These mental monsters are quite good at creeping back without our seeing them. So whenever you find yourself doubting your abilities again, repeat the process. Say goodbye to Doubt and call on Belief to guard your back.

Life is a travelling to the edge of knowledge, then a leap taken.

D. H. LAWRENCE, NOVELIST AND POET (1885–1930)

Just as a cat trusts her instincts and impulses when she jumps, you have to trust yourself in order to make a leap. You have to trust in your abilities, your possibilities and the hard work you've done. The more you believe in yourself, the more others will, too.

Exercise: Get rid of your monsters

Like 'Doubt', pick something that is keeping you from leaping. Maybe it's fear, laziness or low self-esteem. Perhaps it's lack of skills or ambition. Pick something that you know is present and hampering your progress.

Now take out a sheet of paper and draw this creature. Have fun with the drawing, and try to make it symbolize what it means to you. Is it a big ogre or is it thousands of tiny spiders crawling over you? Does it have a sweet face that lulls you into thinking it's your friend? You can make it anything you want. You don't have to be an artist; no one has to see this drawing.

When you've finished, thank the creature and send it on its way. Visualize it leaving. Then flush the drawing down the toilet, or burn it in the fireplace. Get rid of that monster!

Repeat this with other mental monsters until you feel you are free to take some chances and make a leap.

Lesson 8

Heavy petting

I t's easy to show love for your cat. You pet, brush and feed him. You let him fall asleep in your lap, and you always have time to give him a scratch behind the ears. You speak to him in that special voice reserved just for him. And his purring response makes you smile every time.

It would be quite a world if everyone treated humans in the same way, wouldn't it? Granted, not everyone likes to be brushed, but gentle stroking is really quite popular! So why is it so much easier to show your cat constant affection, than the people you love?

One reason is the nature of the relationship. Your love for your cat isn't complicated by the past. He never said something that hurt your feelings, or made you feel unimportant, or had his eyes stray to another human with the message, 'I want her to be my owner instead!' If you get angry at your cat it's for simple reasons. 'Don't jump on the TV!' And you've probably worked out a way to curb that behaviour.

Complicated love

With humans, it's complicated. There are all these large brains, each with their own agendas, their own pasts and their own insecurities. Every time two humans try to accept each other unconditionally, various obstacles arise and mingle, creating barriers that have to be overcome. Sometimes, the difficulties are too great and animosity is the result. But everything becomes worth it when the hurdles are jumped and two people find common ground. That's where love can begin.

Most likely, you've experienced moments of pure, unconditional love for some of the people in your life. If you have children, the moment of their birth is a perfect example. That tiny life, so new and fresh and dependant entered the world and you fell instantly in love. Whether you're a father or a mother, the birth parents or adoptive, the only thing that mattered in those first moments was the love you felt.

A healthy spirit needs love. Grab a piece of paper and jot down the names of six people you love. Done? First question: is your name on that list? Why not? Self-love is one of the keystones of a fulfilling, successful, healthy life. You need to love yourself, if you're going to be able to love others.

If we treated everyone we meet with the same affection

we bestow upon our favourite cat, they, too, would purr.

MARTIN BUXBAUM, AUTHOR AND POET (B. 1912)

Love is a fruit in season at all times, and within reach of every hand.

MOTHER TERESA, CATHOLIC NUN AND NOBEL LAUREATE (1910–1997)

Self-love

One way to show self-love is to stop the constant barrage of negative thoughts. 'I'm a fat pig.' 'I can never do anything right.' 'I'm so stupid.' 'Why don't I ever finish anything I start?' and so on. It doesn't do a thing to help you; it only hurts you. From now on, each time you have a negative thought about yourself, try to work out where it came from, and how to make it positive. Treat yourself as well as you treat your cat, with soft words and gentleness. If a negative thought sneaks through, recognize it and turn it around – make it into a positive affirmation. Self-love could become your greatest asset towards achieving a healthy spirit.

Look at your list again. When was the last time you told those six people that you loved them? I'm talking about saying the actual words with genuine feeling, not 'Oh, he knows I do' or a phrase said by habit, like saying 'hello' or 'goodbye'. It can mean a lot to hear those words. Why not give it a shot? Make a few phones calls and let those people know that someone is thinking about them with warmth and love.

Cats are independent creatures in the wild. They have very little contact with other cats, so that they can keep their territories free from competing predators. But there are some cats upon whom they lavish attention: their mothers and, if female, their kittens. It's a matter of debate whether cats think of their human as a parent or a child. Perhaps it's a mixture of both.

You've probably noticed that when your cat is being stroked and shown a lot of affection, she will occasionally start kneading you with her front paws. This is a kitten behaviour, used when nursing. Kittens knead their mothers to help the milk flow. It's easy to surmise that your cat thinks of you as a parent when she begins this behaviour.

Sometimes, cats will share their prey with you. More than one owner has found a little 'gift' from their cat. A dead mouse makes a lovely surprise in the bed. In the wild, the only time a cat ever shares its prey is when a mother presents it to her young. In this way, your cat is seeing you as its kitten. She's taking care of you by feeding you a mouse.

Both of these behaviours are displays of the love your pet has for you. They show trust, nurturing, and a desire that you understand how important you are to them. Take this wonderful example and show the people you care about how much you love them. Granted, a dead mouse probably won't be all that appreciated, so don't try to be too much like your cat. Pay attention to the message, not the means. Your loved ones deserve a little lavishing.

Exercise: **Love letters**

It's time to write some love letters. Think of three people who mean a great deal to you. It can be a parent, a spouse, a child, a friend, a co-worker, a teacher – anyone. Write each person a letter, telling them the influence they've had on your life, the positive things they mean to you, and the reason they hold such a dear place in your heart.

Tell them about their strengths, and the things you admire about them. Tell them how their words and actions helped make you a better person. Use anecdotes from your shared past to illustrate the impact they have had on you and your life. Let them know how you've used the things they taught you in your life's journey. Be raw and honest and let the words flow from your heart and spirit.

Next, write a similar letter to yourself. Tell yourself all the good things that you can think of. Concentrate on the positive aspects without thought of the negative. Negative is easy. This is a time for deep, searching praise of who you are.

You cannot be lonely if you like the person you're alone with.

DR WAYNE W. DYER, AUTHOR, SPEAKER AND PSYCHOTHERAPIST (B. 1940)

Lesson 9
Shedding

B eing an overly indulgent cat mama, I brush my cat several times a day. It's good for her coat, helps manage shedding, keeps hairballs to a minimum, is a bonding experience, and – oh, let's face it – she has me wrapped around her little paw. I'm powerless when I see those big eyes begging for another round of brushing. She is a hedonist, purring her little heart out with every swipe of the brush. What astonishes me is how much fur comes off each and every time. I could make two cats and a gerbil out of a week's harvest.

Outdoor cats tend to be seasonal in their shedding. Sunlight triggers the hair follicles to grow more during winter, and to shed in summer. Indoor cats, living their lives in artificial light, tend to shed all year long. It can be somewhat mitigated with nutrition and, of course, grooming (constant, constant grooming, if you're in my house), but there's no way to truly control it.

Clutter

Instead of thinking about controlling shedding, think instead of learning from it. It's not a bad idea to shed those things you no longer need. There are hundreds of books written about getting rid of clutter, and most of them speak of it in terms both practical and spiritual.

Physical clutter in your environment is more than an eyesore – it can keep you from bringing new, important things into your life. I always think of clutter as an archaeological dig. There are layers of material, in dated strata, each showing pieces of the past. You can find whole areas that typified a point in your life – the music you listened to, the books you read, the hobbies you enjoyed, the people you considered too close to lose.

In an untouched pile of papers there can be old bills, letters, cards, notes and to-do lists next to receipts, magazines and doodles. Looking through these you can remember your life, what was worrying you, what was exciting you, what was important and what was meaningless.

By holding on to things like this, you are keeping the past alive. It's almost a physical barrier to the present and the future. If you've filled up the empty spaces with things that are no longer important, where will you find room to put the new, exciting things in your life?

It's time to let go. Start sorting through the clutter, making piles of things you want to keep and want to let go. Be willing to be sparing with the first pile, and generous with the second. After all, if you haven't looked for something in several months, why would you still need it?

Life clutter

You might be thinking, 'I don't have that problem. I don't allow clutter in my home.' That's wonderful. But are you truly free of it? You may not have a problem with physical clutter, but it can take other forms as well.

For example, if you're overweight, that's a form of clutter. You're hanging on to food you ate a long time ago. Weight is also a barrier. It's a kind of insular protection against hurt that is too painful to face. Shedding pounds is as necessary as a cat shedding her fur. You need to face whatever hurt caused you to self-medicate with food. Then let go of meals you no longer remember, so that you have room for fresh, nourishing food instead.

Relationships can be clutter, as well. You might be hanging on to an old friendship that is no longer serving you. Instead of warmth, you may feel a building resentment. You may have once loved this person, and needed him as he needed you. But sometimes, it's important to move on.

You might have cluttered emotions. The hurts experienced in childhood are extremely difficult to escape. You might be hanging on to these negative emotions, letting them colour every phase of your adult life without even realizing why certain things make you feel so bad. It's time to examine these feelings, learn whatever lessons they were meant to teach, then let them go.

Freedom from clutter

Shedding can be painful, but it is also very freeing. In the warmth of summer, your cat doesn't need her thick winter coat. Imagine if she refused to let it go. She would swelter, and lose her energy and her playfulness. Her existence would be nothing but heat, merely surviving each day. Negative relationships are like that. They are a burden, and they bring you down, sapping your strength.

You might be someone who hates her job. That, too, can be shed. It's not easy, and it involves some risk, but you spend so much of your day working, that it is a terrible trap if it brings you only unhappiness. You know how to spot opportunities and make the leap. If it's your job that needs to be shed, consider doing something about it, rather than continuing to suffer each day in a heavy coat under a hot sun.

To make room for any improvement in your life, anything new and exciting, you must let go of the things that present a barrier. Whether it's material possessions, excess weight, negative relationships, unhealthy memories and emotions or a dead-end job, it's time to start shedding.

Exercise: Getting rid of clutter

Learn to let go. If you live with too much clutter, pick one area to clean thoroughly. Throw away anything you haven't looked at or cared about for the past few months, and sell what's valuable or donate it to charity. Try to do this every day for the next week. With every rubbish bag you throw out, take a deep breath and let go of everything inside of it.

If you have cluttered emotions, relationships, a job you dislike, or any other sources of mental, emotional or spiritual clutter, decide whether they are serving you or not. By divesting yourself of this negative clutter, you will open yourself to new – more positive – emotions, relationships, jobs, and so on. It takes strength, but it is one of the most worthwhile things you can do to improve the health of your spirit.

Seasons don't make cats shed. Shedding is caused by white fur coming in contact with dark evening clothes.

ANONYMOUS

Lesson 10

Learn to purr

Cats purr in a continuous sound while breathing in and out. You're well acquainted with the contented purr of a cat being held or stroked, but they also purr when facing trauma, injury, and even while they are dying. So why do cats purr?

Scientists have found that a cat's purr vibrates between 25 and 150 Hz. Vibrations between 20 and 140 Hz are therapeutic for bone growth, fracture healing, pain relief, swelling reduction, wound healing, muscle growth and repair, tendon repair, mobility of joints and the relief of dyspnoea (a breathing condition). In short, the remarkable healing ability of cats may have its roots in their ability to purr.

It's also been well documented that cat owners tend to have lower blood pressure — especially in the elderly. Holding a purring cat exposes its owner to these same, healing frequencies. But that's only second-hand. Wouldn't it be wonderful if you could purr?

In a way, you can. You have something that has enormous healing power. This remarkable ability can heal wounds that are physical, mental or spiritual, What is this magical gift? Laughter.

Healing laughter

There are many theories as to why laughter affects health. One major benefit is stress reduction. You've more than likely heard about the dangers of high stress. It can lead to high blood pressure, sleeplessness, eating disorders, even to heart attacks and strokes. It makes sense that anything that can reduce stress would be of great benefit.

Laughter reduces the level of certain stress hormones that have detrimental effects on health, such as suppressing the immune system. Laughter also increases natural 'killer cells' that destroy tumours and viruses. It even increases the body's ability to defend against airborne infection.

The effects aren't limited to the physical. There are also obvious mental and emotional benefits. It's difficult to feel bad when you are laughing. Negative emotions can find safe release in a bout of laughter, leaving us feeling cleansed of some of the emotional detritus that builds up in our lives.

Simple joy

But what about your spiritual health? This is when the cat's purr truly teaches a valuable lesson. Let's return to the purr of the contented cat. It doesn't take enormous events to get a cat to purr. It can start from the smallest of things. Your cat may start purring at the mere sight of you, let alone when you are stroking her. It's a wonderfully pure example of finding simple joy.

Simple joy is perhaps the most important thing you can learn from your cat. It's easy to be joyous about enormous life events, such as the birth of a child, a wedding or a promotion. But what about all those small things that make up an ordinary day? There is joy everywhere around you, if only you'll look.

To live a happy and fulfilled life, it is imperative that you learn to recognize simple joys. A birthday card, a funny line on a sitcom, a good sandwich, a book about cats teaching spiritual lessons – anything can give you joy if you allow it.

It requires you to live in every moment of your life, not just the past or the future. It means allowing seemingly inconsequential things to have importance. The miracle is that all these tiny joys add up to an enormous sense of happiness and contentment, without having to achieve every dream. If you can build a stepladder of simple joys on your way to your goals, you'll find that there is as much fulfilment in the journey as in the achievement.

Think about the day you just experienced. Did you see a loved one, have a good lunch, laugh out loud or smile? Did you finish any tasks, accomplish any goals, check off an item on your to-do list or pet your cat? You can fill in what I missed, but the point is that your day was probably filled with simple, happy moments.

Instead of dismissing them as inconsequential, or not worth getting excited about, revel in them. Add them up and appreciate all the good moments of an otherwise ordinary day.

If you're like most people, you get stressed about negative things that happened, or worry about what might happen. 'I don't have enough money!' 'My husband is late again!' 'There's so much traffic!'

Every negative you dwell on takes a tiny bite out of your happiness. It shrinks the forward progress of your spirit. Granted, it isn't practical not to be concerned about the future. And it's a lot to ask for you to ignore the negative things that happen. But most people *do* ignore the positives, if they aren't big enough, or grand enough in scope.

A cat can be trusted to purr when she is pleased, which is more than can be said for human beings.

WILLIAM RALPH INGE, RELIGIOUS LEADER AND AUTHOR (1860–1954)

Happiness is a thing to be practised, like the violin.

SIR JOHN LUBBOCK, AUTHOR AND ESSAYIST (1834–1913)

To embrace simple joy is to embrace all the happiness you can find in each and every minute of your life. It means you need to 'be in the moment' — if you're laughing, revel in the laughter. If you're watching a good movie, let yourself get lost in that world. Don't just eat something to stave off hunger, delight in it — even if it's just a salad or a piece of fruit. Savour the taste, feel it filling you, take satisfaction in it. When you see a friend's face, rejoice in the closeness you share. And when your cat purrs, purr right along with her.

Exercise: **Finding simple joy**

Learn to be joyous. Over the next week, pay attention to your smiles and laughter. Try to pinpoint the source of the simple joy that was reflected on your face, and in your voice. Take each of these moments and savour them, allowing yourself to feel them without pushing them aside.

It might be the sight of your cat sprawled in a funny position. It might be a joke told by an office colleague. It might be a crayon drawing from your child. It can be anything. But instead of letting the feeling pass, celebrate it. Do this as often as you can, and it won't be an 'exercise' any more. It will become a new and better way of living.

Index

Acknowledgements

Every reasonable effort has been made to acknowledge the ownership of copyright material included in this book. Any errors that have inadvertently occurred will be corrected in subsequent editions provided notification is sent to the publisher.

Carnegie, Dale, *How to Win Friends and Influence People*, Holiday House, 1937

Dement, William C., *The Promise of Sleep: A Pioneer in Sleep Medicine Explores the Vital Connection Between Health, Happiness, and a Good Night's Sleep*, Dell, 2000

Dyer, Dr. Wayne W., *10 Secrets for Success and Inner Peace*, Hay House, 2002

Mother Teresa, *No Greater Love*, New World Library, 2003

Schwab, Fred, *The Last Damn Cat Book*, Lyle Stuart Hardcover, 1982

Picture acknowledgements

AKG, London/Helmut Kalle 61

Alamy/Apply Pictures 18, /Bertrand Demee 81, /A. Parada 70, /Chuck Pefley 85, /PH Photo 48, /Mark Scheuern 5

Corbis UK Ltd/ 54, 92, /Bettmann 44, 62, /Cordaiy Photo Library Ltd./Paul Kaye 57, 78, /Julie Habel 51, /Image Source 35, /Roy Morsch 13, 67, /Genevieve Naylor 73, /Cynthia Diane Pringle 39, /Ford Smith 10, 14, /David H. Wells 47

Getty Images 23, 40, 74, /Paul Cherfils 68, /Dennie Cody 52, /Jim Corwin 24, /Stacey Green front cover, /Steven W Jones 17, /Bill Ling 1, 20, /Ian O'Leary 91, /White Packert 2, /Martin Rogers 86, /Carlos Spaventa 36

Photonica/Neo Vision 32

ZEFA/Pinto 28

Executive Editor Brenda Rosen

Managing Editor Clare Churly

Executive Art Editor Sally Bond

Designer Pia Hietarinta for Cobalt id

Senior Production Controller Ian Paton